John C Sundberg

Health Hints for Travelers

John C Sundberg

Health Hints for Travelers

ISBN/EAN: 9783337210090

Printed in Europe, USA, Canada, Australia, Japan

Cover: Foto ©Andreas Hilbeck / pixelio.de

More available books at **www.hansebooks.com**

FOR

TRAVELERS.

BY

JOHN C. SUNDBERG, M. D.

D. G. BRINTON,
115 SOUTH SEVENTH STREET,
PHILADELPHIA.
1884.

PREFACE.

THE object of this book is to teach the traveler to keep himself well, and to help others who are less fortunate. It is bad enough to fall sick at home, but how much worse when among strangers!

Having traveled myself in almost every climate, and in every quarter of the globe, my experience and my profession have induced me to set forth in plain and brief language a number of suggestions which it will be worth while for travelers to remember. I shall be glad to learn of others of a practical nature, and shall be thankful for any such which may be sent me, care of the publisher of this volume.

1884.   JOHN C. SUNDBERG, M. D.

CONTENTS.

(v)

Health Hints for Travelers.

Getting Ready.

Much of the pleasure and some of the safety of a journey depends on how well the tourist prepares himself to take it. Whatever else he leaves undone, there are some points he should religiously attend to. One of these is

Vaccination. Small-pox is such a loathsome disease, so much feared, so prevalent, and withal so easily prevented, that there is no sort of excuse for any civilized man suffering from it. By all means before starting on any journey of length go through the simple process of *revaccination.* It ought to be repeate every four or five years with genuine bovine or pure human virus, it matters not which. Do not be deluded by the sophistical talk of certain crazy heads into the notion that it is needless or injurious. My observation is but that of thousands of experienced physicians, to the effect that Jenner's discovery was the most valuable made during the last century.

Consult your *dentist* before you go. Even a philosopher is upset by a tooth-ache; how much more the sojourner in a strange land! Moreover, the United States has the best dentists in the world, and if you think of visiting a foreign country, you will not be likely to secure as good work as you can at home. Therefore have your teeth put in thorough repair before you buy your ticket.

You will want with you a few simple *medicines*. I append a list of them at the close of this book. Have such of them as you think you may need put up at some druggist's in whose preparations you have confidence. The doctor often gets the blame that belongs to weak and adulterated drugs.

Much baggage is a nuisance. But as a matter of prudence, do not depart without a good umbrella, rubber overshoes, and a rubber gossamer overall, all to keep out the dampness, that foe to health. A rubber air-cushion is frequently a most agreeable addition to one's comfort. These articles take up very little room.

Carry your own toilet articles with you, and *use no others*. It is well to give a wide berth to the public brushes, combs and towels which one finds in American hotels and clubs. (In Europe they never furnish even soap.) Certain very disagreeable skin diseases may be readily transferred by these articles for promiscuous use.

It is also prudent to provide one's self with a *drinking-cup* for use in the cars or elsewhere. Very ugly diseases can be and have been carried from lip to lip by cups and glasses. Not to speak of others equally loathsome, I recall that Dr. Eklund, of Stockholm, in a recent monograph on leprosy, says that a common source of contagion in Norway, unquestionably, is the promiscuous use of drinking-cups, spoons, etc. The same has been said of cholera among the troops in India.

Colored glasses. These are useful in traveling over snow-covered ground when the sun shines bright, for instance, through Norway and Sweden in winter time. They are almost indispensable on the seashore, at sea, and in some parts of the country where the glare of the sun on the white sand is actually blinding.

Hints About Eating and Drinking.

Food. Follow the customs of the country. It is the opinion of some of the highest medical authorities in India, that if the Europeans would adopt the mode of living of the Hindus, viz., abstain from flesh and alcohol, they would be better able to withstand the evil effects of the climate.

The author lives almost exclusively on fruit and milk (when the latter can be obtained) in tropical climates, and even in the temperate and cold countries during summer. During the early part of the summer of 1878, while in Calcutta, where at the time cholera was raging all around, my daily dinner was invariably as follows: One pineapple, two or three mangoes, and a few bananas or other fruit. I was warned strongly by physicians and others against this practice; I, however, kept perfectly healthy, while Europeans and natives died all around me from cholera and sun-

9*

stroke. I think that we should always select fruit
that is perfectly sound, and I would under no circumstances eat any portion of an apple or an orange in
which there was the smallest spot that was beginning
to decay.

Drinks. Water containing organic impurities may
be rendered potable by (1) boiling, (2) filtering
through charcoal, (3) adding a small quantity of per-
manganate of potassium, and letting it stand and
settle.

Alcohol is useful after exposure to severe cold; for
instance, after having been rescued from a wreck at
sea and brought into a warm cabin. The great danger
then is congestion of internal organs, which alcohol
tends to prevent by driving the blood outwards. But
· alcohol is not of the least value while the person is so
exposed; on the contrary, it diminishes the power to
resist cold. It is useful taken in small quantities with
the food while undergoing severe fatigue, though
under such circumstances I have found it inferior to
coffee. Men when about to visit tropical countries
are frequently advised, even by their physician, to
drink brandy freely, and to either abstain from water
entirely, or at least never to take it pure. While on a
visit to Delhi during the winter of 1879, I met there
a well known American gentleman who told me that
he had been warned against the water both of Europe
and the East, and in order to be on the safe side, he
had not, so he said, tasted water since he left Phila-

delphia. A wealthy and refined lady in Ceylon, informed me that as far as she knew she had never tasted pure water, nor did she ever allow her children to drink water without first *diluting* it with brandy.

As a result of this erroneous idea, for which physicians are to a certain extent responsible, I have found that a large number of the English ladies living in India consume daily: Beer 3 pints, claret 3 pints, sherry or champagne 1 pint, brandy from 1 to 4 and even 6 ounces. The men drink, on an average, much more, especially of the brandy, which diluted with an equal part of soda-water is with many a favorite beverage.

The same I have found to be the custom among the Europeans in South America. Is it then any wonder that many of these climates exert such evil influences on the system in general, and the liver in particular? As a proof that alcohol is not needed in tropical climates any more than in the temperate, let me state the case of an American gentleman, the Rev. Dr. J. Phillips, total abstainer, who had lived in Arissa for nearly forty years, and had undergone a great amount of hardships and exposure in this home of malaria, and yet retained a vigorous body almost up to his death, which occured at the advanced age of 69. Whenever I have, in the tropics or elsewhere, met a temperate man, I have usually found him to be healthy, and better able to undergo hardships than he who is habituated to the daily use of stimulants.

"Every man," says the eminent Dr. Parkes, in his treatise on *Hygiene*, "who examines the subject in good faith, is the best judge of the exact diet which suits him." The general rule is that the amount of food should be in proportion to the amount of exercise taken. But the trouble is to get persons to use their own best judgment about satisfying their appetite. Dr. Parkes says in another passage, that even to-day, thirty per cent. of those who consult a physician owe their diseases in some way to their diet!

It is a good habit to take a reasonable amount of fluid before starting in the morning, and very little during the day. Of the many excellent reasons for keeping the mouth shut, one is that it lessens greatly the sense of thirst. A piece of onion, a grain of cayenne pepper, a trifle of spice, still better a fragment of slippery elm bark, will allay thirst without the use of water.

In India, travelers carry a "filtering stone," with tube attached. In default of some such simple apparatus, suspicious drinking water should be boiled and cooled. At hotels, some of the numerous natural mineral waters can nearly always be obtained, and they are often preferable to the local water.

Washing and Bathing.

Cleanliness is praiseworthy and salutary, but there is not much wisdom in universal cold bathing—"tub-bing," as the English call it. A cold bath, by which

I mean one when the temperature of the water is anywhere below 70° Fah., requires a solid constitution to resist its dangers. Drs. Martin and Mosely pronounce it "eminently unsafe" to the aged, the very young, to the debilitated, the intemperate, to those suffering from any organic disease, and—especially noteworthy here— to those who have recently undergone any great fatigue of mind or body. The warm bath—from 85° to 95°— is safe to all.

An excellent substitute for the bath is the *flesh brush*. After one becomes accustomed to it, it is a delightful implement and indispensable toilet article. Pains and aches disappear before it "like magic," as the patent medicine men say. It is cleanly, handy, portable, stimulating and soothing, all in one.

A rough towel or the flesh gloves are next in value, but a long way behind.

The Weather, Air and Ventilation.

When the heat is excessive, there are many ways of cooling the rooms. Pankhas, which are immense fans suspended under the ceiling, will be found delicious, and in the case of hot winds, such as prevail in the northwest provinces of India during March, April, May, and June, a wet screen (tatti), suspended before the doors and windows, through which the wind is allowed to pass, will make a person coming from without imagine that he is approaching the north pole. Americans do not as a rule pay enough attention to the art of keeping cool in hot weather. Travelers should provide themselves with sun hats (solar topies) and white umbrellas.

Wet Clothing.—If wet from salt water, no harm will come from it. I was once wet night and day, sleeping and awake, for six weeks, with a temperature near and at times below the freezing point, but was none the worse for it at the end of that time.

Cold Weather.—Although the winter temperature of Norway and Sweden is usually very severe, sometimes falling below the freezing point of mercury, I never remember to have suffered much from cold, although I have spent nineteen winters in Norway. With the intense cold there is usually a perfect calm with dryness of the atmosphere (this only applies to the interior, not to the coast), hence the great tolerance. I once as a boy walked 210 English miles in six days, in a temperature which during that time ranged from twenty to thirty degrees Fah. below zero. I kept my ears and nose warm by rubbing them frequently with snow.

Choosing a Room.

Always select a room on the sunny side of the house, even in the tropics. It has been found in India, that the mortality is less among the soldiers who occupy the south side of the barracks.

A word about *respirators*. They are useful in dense, dank, penetrating fogs, in smoky, gassy places, on very dusty roads, in raw winds, and to all whose throat and lungs are threatened. The simplest is a silk handkerchief placed over the nostrils and mouth, and it is astonishing how much comfort this often gives. Of the permanent kind, a thin slice of clean close-grained sponge (half an inch thick), will answer very well. In India they extemporize an efficient disinfecting respirator by enclosing a layer of fresh charcoal in cotton. Various others are manufactured, especially in London, where they are much more used than in this country.

Hygiene of Railway Traveling.

Some writers on sanitary science have framed a formidable bill of indictment against railways, on the score of the injury they do to health. The surgeons of the hospitals of Paris and Lyons found nearly seven per cent. of the engineers and firemen suffering from affections of the brain and nervous system, owing principally to their occupation. Dr. Blyth, in his "Dictionary of Hygiene," accuses the waiting-rooms at stations of being "nothing more or less than centres for the propogation of typhoid fever and similar diseases." The frequent exposure to drafts is also very injurious. As an English writer observes: "One may live in a pest-house for years; but to be suddenly cooled down to an easily-reached point, puts us in a few minutes beyond all help, and a draft may bring death like a bullet."

Drafts, in fact, are one of the greatest dangers in railway traveling. They may produce catarrhal affections, sore throat, earache, toothache, pleurisy, pneumonia— a long train of ills. They are increased with the rapidity of the train, and whenever the temperature of the air is below 65°, they have all the dangerous properties of a "cold draft." It is well to remember that in cold weather there is much less risk from foul air than from open windows, and the safer rule is to *keep the car-windows shut*. As a safeguard against drafts, I particularly recommend persons to carry a blanket, or a "railway rug," to wrap around their legs and feet. The philosophy of this is that the first effect of a general chill is to drive the blood from the extremities (the arms and legs and feet) to the central organs, and hence the importance of keeping these extremities protected and warm. If in spite of care, a generally chilly feeling is experienced, the best remedy is immediately to swallow a quarter or an eighth of a grain of morphia, or one grain of opium, or twenty drops of laudanum. I know a very eminent surgeon who tells me that for years on his frequent journeys he has invariably carried such morphine pills for this purpose.

Nausea and sick feelings, with faintness, are produced in many persons by the movement of a rapid train. The sensation is something like sea-sickness, and is probably caused by the jolting of the intestines and gall bladder. Dr. Walter Lewis, the Medical Superintendent of the London Post-office, has observed this so often in "bilious" persons, that he now rejects them as unfit for the traveling service of the postal department. The best preventative of this unpleasant effect is to tie a bandage tightly around the abdomen, and to carry a small vial of chloroform, of which a few whiffs should be sniffed up when the sensations come on.

The headache produced in some persons by railway traveling, is sometimes brought about by the noise and vibration of the cars acting on the *ears*. I have heard of one case where it was entirely prevented by filling the ears with cotton, before entering the cars. In others, we must look to the *eyes* for its cause. These organs are more or less tried by the rapid recurrence of momentary impressions on the retina. Any one can test this for himself by trying to count the fence-posts when the train is in rapid motion. Persons whose eyes are weak experience the same disagreeable strain from looking out in the ordinary manner.

Dryness of the throat, passing sometimes into troublesome irritation of the vocal organs, is quite common with susceptible people who try to talk in the cars. The cause of it is two-fold; first, because in order to drown the noise of the train they have to pitch the voice in an unusual key, which strains the vocal cords; and secondly, because the air in long railway journeys has a drying effect both on the skin and mucous membrane, and renders them unusually sensitive. The prevention is simple: do not converse in the cars, and *keep your mouth shut.*

In spite of the ingenuity which has been expended upon the subject, the *dust* remains one of the greatest annoyances in railway traveling.   It is extremely irritating both to the eyes and the breathing passages. Many experienced travelers protect the eyes by "goggles;" ladies can use veils, which are, however, unpleasant in hot weather.   A respirator will protect the breathing passages, if it seems advisable to have recourse to it.

Hints for Traveling with Infants.

Every traveler knows the horror of the squalling baby in the crowded car.   The poor little things suffer much, but most of their misery and that of their traveling companions could be avoided by timely precautions.

One of the greatest troubles is about their food and drink.   I recommend decidedly the use of *condensed milk* on journeys with small children.   The tin being opened before starting, and a little of the milk taken out to prevent any running over, it is placed carefully in an ordinary small traveling provision-basket, not in a hand-bag.   It is better to have a teaspoon as well, so that the quantity may be easily measured.   Children, even if they are not accustomed to this kind of milk, take it readily, and digest it well.   Even though the tin be left open, the milk remains perfectly good during the longest journey.

The next difficulty is in providing hot water to mix

with the milk, or in heating the mixture to a proper
temperature without the trouble and risk of boiling it
over a spirit-lamp every time the child needs the bottle.
This may readily be avoided by the following expedi-
ents.

An ordinary stone bottle, such as is commonly employed in winter to place at the foot of the bed to keep
the feet warm, holding about half a gallon of water, is
first wrapped round with several thicknesses of sheet
cotton-wadding, the ends being brought round so as to
entirely encircle the bottle.   Outside this, two or three
yards of stout house-flannel are wound, and fastened
securely by a needle and thread, the ends being
gathered in, as in the case of the wadding.   The
flannel and wadding are, of course, cut so as to allow
the neck of the bottle to protrude.   To improve the
appearance of the whole, a piece of scarlet flannel is
then neatly sewn on, and an ordinary rug-strap, with a
handle, adjusted, so as to allow portability.   A few
hours before starting, the bottle must be filled with
nearly boiling water, and the cork, which must be perfectly clean, or the screw-stopper, adjusted.   The
object of doing this is to heat thoroughly the bottle
and its coverings.   Shortly before starting, the bottle
is first emptied, and then again filled with fresh boiling
water.   This can be readily carried by the aid of the
strap without any inconvenience whatever.   If properly
prepared, the water, which at the time of starting is at
a temperature of about 200° Fahr., will remain con-

siderably over 100°, even though the quantity is constantly being diminished, for a period of twelve to six-
teen hours.

Children who have only recently given up the use
of the bottle are still dependent to a great extent upon
liquid food, though it is not always necessary in hot
weather that the food should be warm. For this reason, a bottle of milk and another of plain· water should
form part of the traveling-basket. Children suffer
much from thirst, as a rule, when travelling; and, if
milk be given to them undiluted, it tends to increase,
and not to satisfy, this craving for liquid. Plain water,
in small quantities, at appropriate intervals, allays
thirst, and prevents children from being so restless and
irritable.

In place of buns, cakes, and sweet crackers, it is far
better to take only plain water-crackers, thin slices of
bread and butter, carefully packed in a sandwich-tin, or
even simple crusts of bread, which do not provoke
thirst as in the case of sweet things. Egg-sandwiches,
made with eggs not boiled too hard, prove an useful
addition on long journeys, and are much relished by
young children as well as by adults. Ripe fruit, to a
moderate amount, is also very grateful, where children
are old enough to be indulged with it.

Children who are unused to traveling often have a
great dread of the whistling of the engine as it enters
a tunnel, or rushes swiftly past some station with gas-
lamps flaring along its whole length. To obviate

these, a little cotton-wool, lightly packed at the orifice of the ear, gently pressed into the external meatus only sufficiently far to prevent the wool from actually falling out, and the precaution of drawing the blind or the curtains across the car windows, will prove of great service.

It is a mistake to wrap up children too much when traveling in summer; the unusual clothing only irritates them, and makes them restless and peevish, preventing their sleeping, and causing unnecessary discomfort.

In cases were children are exceedingly nervous and excitable, readily frightened, and unable to sleep when traveling, a dose of five or ten grains of the bromide of potassium, depending upon the age of the child is often of service in restraining undue excitement and ensuring sleep.

Tours Afoot.

The earliest, and still in many respects often the most pleasant mode of travel, is to go afoot. It is the only way in which the full attraction of beautiful scenery can be appreciated. One escapes the annoyance of hurrying by charming views, and it is reserved for the pedestrian alone to gain a real acquaintance with the people of the land through which he travels. Some adopt foot traveling from necessity, quite as many from pleasure. Not many years ago an English physician was thoughtful enough to make a careful collection of the medical and hygienic hints which are suitable to the pedestrian, and I shall repeat, in the main, the judicious advice of Dr. Watson, adding to it various suggestions from the experience of myself and others.

TRAINING BEFOREHAND.

For some days before setting out on a foot journey, the tourist should practice regular training, beginning with moderate walks, and increasing them daily. This serves also to break in the shoes, and to harden the feet. The body also must be brought into good condition. A warm bath with thorough towelling repeated several times, opens the pores of the skin and relieves the internal organs. A gentle dose of laxative medicine, as of one of the aperient mineral waters now to be found in every drug-store, is also a useful preliminary. If the diet has been rich and full, it should be moderated.

PREPARING THE FEET.

Comfort, pleasure, success, everything about a foot tour, depends on the condition of the feet. A corn, a chafed heel, a hang nail will destroy all the charms of scenery and joy of companionship. The most scrupulous precautions to avoid such petty evils are never excessive or beneath respect.

THE NAILS.

If the toe-nails are suffered to grow too long, they have a tendency to curve downward and inward, some-

times growing into the flesh, or causing discomfort by
the pressure of the upper leather of the shoe.

They must not, however, be cut too short, as this in
turn prevents them from being what they by nature
are, a defence to the extremely sensitive extremities of
the toes.

The proper length to keep them is so that the edge
of the nail is a line or two behind the extreme end of
the toe. It is quite important to cut them *square*, not
rounded or *en amande*, as the French say, as the latter
plan favors their growing into the flesh and cutting the
skin in walking.

This accident of *ingrown toe-nail* is one of the most
obstinate and painful of all the affections of the foot.
It is usually the big toe which is the sufferer. The
corner of the nail is forced into the flesh, bleeding and
irritation follow, and sometimes actual and severe lame-
ness are produced in consequence.

This accident may be *prevented* by close attention to
the condition of the nails, and by cutting them square.
If any irritation or chafing by the edge of the nail
against the flesh is perceived, a narrow strip of isinglass
plaster must be inserted beneath the nail and carried
firmly around the toe over the irritated edge of flesh,
thus interposing this protective barrier between the
nail and the flesh. The corner of the nail must *not* be
cut off. That were bad treatment. But the convex
portion or back of the nail may be scraped thin with a
piece of glass or knife edge from the root to the free

edge. This weakens and flattens the arch of the nail,
so that the borders do not press so firmly on the flesh
at the sides.   Some cotton may also be pressed under
the edges of the nail, to lift them up and away from the
flesh.

CORN DOCTORING.

In every city in the United States corn extractors,
or as they prefer to be called, chiropodists or pedicures, are to be found.   It is fair to say that as a rule
they have a good deal of practical skill, and their
services will repay, in increased comfort, the moderate
charges they usually make.   To a sufferer from corns
a few dollars now and then are well laid out in having
these artists remove the callosities and redress the
irregularities of his feet.   Before starting on a pedestrian excursion, it would be well to have one's services.

As, however, not all have the chance and others will
not recollect or care to take this advice, I add directions for treating corns independently of pedicures.

First, to relieve them.   To do this, soak them a few
minutes in warm water, apply a drop of sweet-oil, and
then cut them down carefully, being very careful not
to draw blood, as this sometimes results in producing
ugly sores.   Soap the cut surface a little, and touch it
lightly with a stick of *fused nitrate of silver* (lunar
caustic).   After a few minutes wipe off the soap, and
cover with a piece of sticking plaster or lead plaster
spread on linen. , Be careful not to apply the caustic

beyond the hard, horny spot, or a sore may be produced.

This method does very well to produce temporary relief, but not a cure, as the so-called "root" or stem of the corn remains, and for a cure this must be extracted. This can be done by any tolerably skillful and patient person. A penknife with a rather dull blade, or a sharp-pointed bodkin, is required. Softening the core with a drop of oil, the operator digs or scratches cautiously round and round the root, loosening it by degrees from its bed, going slowly deeper and deeper, until the whole root is thus exposed. It may then be removed by a small pair of forceps. If properly done, this operation is entirely *painless* and entirely *bloodless*.

After the root is removed, pressure on the spot should not cause the least pain. The part should be covered with a plaster, and the toe bound up for a few days.

More serious annoyance of similar character is caused by

BUNIONS.

Under this name are popularly included two very different complaints. Thus I find several works addressed to pedestrians describing a bunion as "a many-stemmed corn situated over or on the outer side of the large joint of the great toe." It is true that large multiple corns are frequently produced at these spots by ill-fitting shoes, and on account of their size and exposed situation are peculiarly apt to become inflamed and painful. The bending of the joint at every step aggravates the soreness and hinders recovery.

This sort of bunion is, however, nothing more than an exaggeration of an ordinary corn, and the directions I have above given will apply to the treatment of such a callosity quite well.

Very different and much more serious is the ailment which surgeons call a bunion. This is nothing else than a chronic inflammation and consequent enlargement of the principal joint of the great toe. It is usually caused by wearing a shoe which is too short, and thus presses the toe back against the corresponding bone of the foot, not giving the joint sufficient play, and exciting inflammation of one or both its articular surfaces.

Here no domestic remedy will avail, nor need an immediate recovery be expected at the most skillful hands. A wide shoe, and a proper splint and bandage, will have to be worn for a long time to restore the joint to a state of health. But as a pedestrian journey cannot be contemplated by such a sufferer, I need not enter further into this matter.

FOOT SORENESS, CHAFING AND BLISTERING.

These are the commonest annoyances when journeying afoot. They may be generally avoided by securing a well-fitting shoe, and having it gradually broken in, and well oiled. The stockings should be free from creases and seams, and preferably of soft wool. After some hours' walking, when the feet are beginning to feel hot, chafed and sore, the stockings should be changed from one foot to the other, or turned inside out, so that the point of pressure will be relieved.

But the most efficient preservative is to have the feet well greased before starting out. Some pedestrians prefer for this purpose neats-foot oil; others use tallow or washed lard; others say nothing equals the yolk of an egg; while others again believe in soaping the inside of the stocking with common yellow hard soap, making a good lather, and rubbing it in. Probably it makes little difference which of these plans is adopted, the end gained being the same in all; so I will leave if to the fancy and convenience of the reader to select for himself.

When a blister is once formed, do not open it. That is the worst measure to take. It is painful at the time, and the foot grows sore afterwards. Get a needleful of silk or worsted; pass it through the blister; tie the two ends together and leave the thread in; the next morning cut off both ends with the scissors, leaving the thread in the now drained and flattened blister undisturbed.

Another plan, much used by Swiss travelers, is to rub the blistered part gently for some time on going to bed with spirits mixed with tallow dropped from a candle into the palm of the hand. The next morning no blister remains.   This has the endorsement of many distinguished pedestrians.

When the shin has been broken and a chafed, sore, raw surface has been formed, very considerable comfort may be regained by covering it smoothly with one or two layers of court plaster.   No pedestrian should start out without a piece of this simple and valuable substance with him.   He will probably bless its dis-coverer more warmly than Sancho Panza did the inventive genius who first discovered sleep.

At night, chafed and inflamed surfaces should be well greased, or else covered with a clay poultice—a simple remedy, very generally at hand, and very cool-ing, grateful and healing to most inflamed parts.

WASHING AND BATHING THE FEET.

There is a difference of opinion among professed pedestrians as to the propriety of using much water to the feet when on a long tramp.   The medical regula-tions of the British army in India are emphatic that the feet should not be washed with cold water when long marches are contemplated.   Some authorities disap-prove of much washing with any kind of water.   The natural oily secretion of the skin is removed by the fluid, and consequently cracks, chafes and blisters are more liable to occur.   Wiping with a damp towel or sponge, say these writers, is enough for cleanliness.

The counsel that I should give would be to bathe the feet every evening in tepid water, but not to let them soak long; and after wiping them, to rub in some penetrating animal oil, as neat's-foot. This meets the demands of both parties, the advocates of cleanliness and those of oiliness.

The excessive perspiration of the feet with which some persons are annoyed is increased by frequent washing; yet cleanliness is essential to remove the disagreeable odor which always attends this immoderate secretion. The socks should be of woolen, and finely powdered fresh vegetable charcoal should be strewn in the bottom of the shoe to absorb the fetid emanation.

At the end of a day's walk, it is a good rule to take off shoes and stockings, rub the feet with a damp cloth, dry them well, and put on clean, dry stockings and light slippers. Especially is this necessary when the feet are damp, either from rain, stepping in water, or perspiration. Under no circumstances should a person sit with wet feet, or undertake to dry them by sitting in front of a fire.

SHOES AND STOCKINGS.

A great variety of shoes and boots claim the patronage of.the pedestrian. Few of them stand the test of experience. The so-called "Congress shoes," with elastic sides, compress the cords and vessels of the ankle, heat the foot, and impede the circulation. The much extolled "Waukenphast" last, with an almost straight interior border, and narrowed over the toes, is not suitable for long tramps.

A good shoe will fit closely nowhere but on the

instep, where it should exert a firm and equable pressure. It will allow plenty of room for the toes to ex-
pand and extend in every direction, but not enough
for them to rub and slip about or override each other.
The soles should extend beyond the lines of the up-
pers, and the heels be broad and low. The fastenings
should be by laces or strings, which alone allow the
pressure to be accurately adjusted to the thickness of
the stockings and the varying size of the ankle—for
the circumference of the ankle varies considerably after
a period of rest and a number of hours walking, especially in lymphatic persons.

In having a measure taken for a walking shoe, the
circumference of the foot when the weight of the body
is thrown upon it must be taken into account. In
some persons this is almost the same as when at rest;
but in others the increase is twenty to thirty per cent.,
and for such, a shoe fitted to the foot at rest will surely
give annoyance.

In many parts of Europe foot-tourists wear leggins
buttoning from the knee to the ankle, made of soft
leather or corduroy. They protect against mud and
wet, and relieve the nuisance of the pantaloons flapping
against the shins. More devoted pedestrians adopt
regular Knickerbockers or knee-breeches, with heavy
woolen hose. During our war the daily experience
of long marches taught our infantry the convenience
of such a costume, and they extemporized it by tuck-
ing the ends of their pantaloons into their stockings.

Nearly all authorities advocate socks or stockings of wool—thick, soft, lamb's-wool, without seams or ribs. To some skins, especially in warm weather, the feel of woolen is irritating and disagreeable. Such may draw on a thin cotton sock under the woolen; or well made smooth and soft cotton hose may answer as well. Any kind that appears to increase the liability to blistering should be discarded.

Whatever hose are worn, the *garter* should be dispensed with. Not only does the constriction of the extremity it causes produce swelling and heating of the feet, varicose veins, and other local difficulties, but the disturbance thus introduced into the general circulation has been proven at times to be the exciting agency of headaches and general malaise. The male sex can employ half-hose; while the ladies can adopt the plan now advocated by the "dress reform" teachers, of suspending the stockings from a waist-belt.

A PEDESTRIAN'S COSTUME.

A due regard to comfort and health will lead the pedestrian to dress in woolen garments, light or heavy, according to the season of the year. The outfit that Dr. Watson recommends in his useful little book entitled "Hints to Pedestrians," is a shooting jacket of Scotch plaid or tweed, a double-breasted waistcoat, loose pantaloons, a light cap and a flannel shirt. Probably a soft felt hat is superior to a cap. In the heats of summer a ventilating hat, or Indian helmet, is altogether advisable.

A practiced pedestrian will not wear a rubber or other water-proof coat. Even the lightest are too hot and uncomfortable. A square piece of rubber cloth to throw over the knapsack, or with a slit in the centre to be worn as a poncho, is far more useful than a coat. With this, an umbrella may be dispensed with; but the umbrella in turn may be a grateful adjunct for its shade in walking over a sunny road in hot weather.

The baggage should be light, not exceeding 15 or 18 pounds. Some prefer to carry it in pouch, fishing basket, or game-bag at the side; but a well-fitting knapsack distributes the weight more agreeably. To prevent the unpleasant heating of the back from a knapsack, they may now be had resting on a frame of basket-work which allows the free circulation of the air between the weight and the body.

A well-made umbrella will serve all the purposes of a cane. The best shaft is one of reed, which is both light and strong. The handle should be at right angles to the shaft, or slightly curved. The steel ribs and iron ferule of an umbrella have been accused of attracting lightning, and thus adding to the dangers of a thunder-storm. I mention this, though it is difficult to believe that there is any actual peril in using them.

HOW MANY MILES A DAY.

Mr. Ruskin gives it as his opinion that properly to enjoy and appreciate scenery, the tourist afoot should not walk more than a dozen miles a day. The hygienist will agree that for the first day or two this should not be much exceeded. The stress and strain of the journey are in the first three days. These victoriously past, the exercise becomes much easier. Anything like a "spurt" is unwise.

It is justly remarked by a writer on this subject that to push the daily journey to the point of great fatigue, so as to render the muscles sore and trembling, and stiff and painful after a night's rest, is to dispel both pleasure and benefit. We might say that on an average a dozen or fifteen miles will be enough for the first day's walk. If they rest well the following night and rise refreshed the next morning, they can add five miles the second day, and a day or two later increase this to five-and-twenty miles. The warning is useful, however, that whenever the pedestrian finds his appetite diminished, his sleep restless, or a sense of exhaustion the next morning, he should promptly lessen his daily stint.

With regard to meals and meal-times the old rule is a good one, "light food before the journey and solid food after it." I should recommend however that some food always be taken before setting out in the morning. It is a fact well known to all physicians that a person is much more liable to contagious and infectious diseases when the stomach is empty than when it is full. Malarial poison is more active in the early morning than later in the day; therefore the tourist who begins his walk before breakfast runs a double risk of being affected by any dangerous exhalation prevalent.

2*

No meals should be taken immediately after arriving at a place of rest, nor should the walk be resumed until at least half an hour after the meal is finished.

TO REMOVE THE MUSCULAR SORENESS

which follows over-exertion in walking, climbing, etc., the most effective measure is to take a hot bath and then to jump into a well-warmed bed. Sponging well with hot water and rubbing the sorest parts with tincture of arnica are also useful, and take the place of the hot bath.

Equestrian Tours.

That noble animal, the horse, offers a means of conveyance to the tourist now fallen into much disuse in fully civilized countries, but still indispensable over vast areas of the earth's surface. In South America and Asia, the horse, the mule, or the camel, is still almost the only, certainly the customary carrier. It would be well for many invalids to turn their attention to horseback exercise as a means of restoration to health. I find in my note-book the opinion of some physician in these words: " Peruvian bark is no surer cure for ague than riding is for consumption." That is saying too much. But the truth remains that in the early stages of this justly-dreaded disease, riding, combined with the observance of sound hygienic precepts, offers a very good chance, indeed, to escape the otherwise almost inevitable results.

But equestrian exercise may do also a great deal of

harm, if unwisely pursued, or in certain constitutions. Thus I have heard of a case where a person riding rapidly against a strong wind brought on a severe attack of hemorrhage from the lungs. Asthmatic persons are often much distressed by the motion. Those who suffer from piles will aggravate their disease by horse-back riding. Those who have any tendency to rupture will incur considerable danger by the jolting. Where there is an aneurism, a fatal injury may be produced by the same cause. And finally, in all acute diseases, the motion is altogether too violent for safety.

Those who would take an equestrian tour should practice gradually for at least a month before they start, or else pleasure and benefit will be seriously jeopardized. On the road, they should avoid the saddle immediately after meals, as the pressure of the abdominal muscles sometimes causes regurgitation and vomiting. A light rubber overcoat is indispensable to protect one from the weather. The saddle should be selected with the utmost care, with a view to ease in riding, and also to the avoidance of galling the animal's back.

At Sea.

The hints which will be serviceable to the traveler by sea, will differ somewhat depending on whether he goes by sail or by steam; but in some respects he will have the same difficulties to encounter and the same maladies to guard against. The most certain and perhaps the most disagreeable of these will be

SEA-SICKNESS.

This is a terror to many, and a most serious discomfort to nearly all who go down to the sea in ships. I may as well say at the outset that there is no sure cure for it, not even any very certain alleviative. Yet there are some practical suggestions that will prove of decided service to those who are liable to this complaint. Some of these suggestions have recently been thrown into a condensed form in a book on ocean traveling by Dr. W. S. Wilson, a London physician of wide nautical experience.

He urges the invalid first of all not to make the mistake of supposing that sea-sickness is an unmitigated evil. Dr. Wilson maintains that it is within moderate limits decidedly beneficial, and an admirable if not indispensable preparation for receiving the full benefits of a sea voyage. He adds that it is very seldom prejudicial to health, and that even those who suffer from it most severely enjoy more than their usual health shortly after reaching land.

It can undoubtedly be diminished in severity by a preparation of the general system for a few days before embarking. This preparation should consist in considerable moderation in diet, and the use of some aperient medicine such as the laxative mineral waters.

When the nausea commences, a bandage such as a handkerchief firmly fastened around the waist will sometimes afford considerable personal relief. Very many medicines have been suggested from time to time, such as chloroform, chloral, bromide of potassium, and the like. One of the latest is nitro-glycerine, which is prepared in tablets pleasant to the palate, and is reported to give decided relief in about half the cases. Experienced ship surgeons, however, such as Dr. Wilson, are of opinion that these agents, although they do relieve for a time, cause more harm than good in the long run. It is the observation of these gentlemen that it is best not to interfere with the complaint by administering drugs.

The wisest plan to pursue is as follows : During the first violence of the attack retire to your berth, and keep as quiet as possible. Endeavor to control the retching by a strong effort of the will. Sleep as much as possible. As the debility from lack of food is one of the most unpleasant features of the disease, nourishment must be taken in small quantities at frequent intervals. No matter if it does excite loathing at first, and is rejected by the stomach, the effort to take it must be continued. Of the forms of nourishment most suitable, I may specify beef-tea perfectly free from fat, or a solution of Liebig's extract. These will rest better on the stomach if either ice cold or very hot. They may be well seasoned with cayenne pepper, which condiment appears at all times to exert a very beneficial effect upon the weakened mucous membrane of the stomach. Indeed, strong cayenne lozenges are about the most useful remedy known for allaying the uncomfortable nausea which sea-sickness leaves behind it.

With reference to stimulants, naval surgeons speak
well of brandy in *very small* quantities well diluted
with soda water, and also a dry champagne well iced.
Less objectionable in some respects, and perhaps
equally efficacious, is the ginger ale now to be had on
most ships.

An important rule is to go on deck as soon as the
sickness has moderately subsided, and to remain in
the open air as much as possible. Those who have
sufficient determination to do this, always make a much
more rapid recovery than those who remain below.

Sea-sickness generally leaves behind it a good deal
of constipation, and a few doses of some mild aperient
medicine will usually be necessary in order to complete the cure.

Traveling in Search of Health.

All that has been said about the care which the
ordinary traveler should exercise to preserve his
health, applies with redoubled force to those whose
prime object in a tour is to recruit an exhausted constitution, or to escape a threatening disease. There
are works written for their especial instruction, which
go at length into the benefit of this and that climate,
this and that health resort, so that I shall not attempt
here to say much on the subject.

But there are several points which I should advise
them very carefully to consider about any locality they
propose to visit. These are:

1. Its climate.
2. The facilities for reaching it and for *getting away again*.
3. What accommodations it offers.
4. What sort of food and cooking one may expect.

All these ought to be decidedly favorable, if the invalid expects to gain the purpose of his journey.

Both on the journey and at its goal, a delicate person should resolutely refuse to sleep in a room on the ground floor, or one that is damp or ill-smelling. They have a pestilent custom in Europe of fumigating a room by burning odoriferous pastilles, done really for the purpose of concealing the noisome odors in it. In choosing a residence, select an open sunny situation with good drainage. In Italy or Florida, a winter room with windows to the south and plenty of air and sunlight is altogether preferable.

My observation of invalids at health-resorts persuades me that many suffer horribly from *ennui*. To meet this, a congenial companion is most effectual. Also, some regular employment, suitable to the case, should be adopted. When out-of-door exercise is possible, collecting in some branch of natural history is an admirable resource. If not, some indoor occupation must be suggested. I know of a very distinguished Chicago merchant who learned to crochet beautifully during a long winter spent at a certain New York spring. He was greatly benefited of the dyspepsia and insomnia that troubled him, and no

doubt this novel occupation had its share in his restoration to health.

The Insect Plagues.

1. *Mosquitoes.*—The worst place, perhaps, in the
world is Archangel, in Russia, during the summer
months; they are so thick that a mosquito-bar is of
no value, as it would be filled before it would be possible to get under. I have tried to keep them off by
beating my face constantly with a towel, but to no
purpose; the only rest I could get was in a hammock
rigged under the main-top-gallant yard of a ship; they
did not follow me so high. The Russians have a
means of keeping them out of their houses, but I
could never learn the secret. The mosquitoes in the
swamps of Louisiana are civil compared to those on
the banks of the Dwina, perhaps because they are
fewer in number.

Against mosquitoes in ordinary numbers, and
against many other plagues of the insect world, a box
of *fresh Persian Insect Powder* is a blessed boon. It
must be fresh and genuine, and I say this because a
large share of that in the market is adulterated or old,
and thus worthless. The fresh powder thrown into
the air of a room will keep mosquitoes at a distance,
and sprinkled rather liberally in and around the bed-
ding will prove highly distasteful to *fleas* and *bedbugs.*

For these pests I find what seems a most efficient
suggestion in a late work by an English traveler. He
introduces it thus:

"In Jerusalem, during the height of summer, I have seen my bed pretty well alive with fleas, and have swept them out with my hands before going to bed. In the excavations or vaults in Mount Moriah, known by the name of 'Solomon's Stables,' I have seen my clothes pretty well covered with them; and in Athens I have witnessed, at the early dawn, the bugs leaving my bed and crawling up the bedposts by the score, '*ne dicam*' by the hundred, and neither place was I bitten once. I adopted the following antidote, formed on what I heard of as being done in Hungary, a land much vexed in the summer-time by fleas, and so on. I oiled myself *all over* from head to foot with the best sweet or olive oil, and those parts of my back that I could not effectually get at myself, I got oiled for me by the help of a friend or of a servant. Rub the oil well in with the palm of your hand over the whole body—head, face, and all—in a warm room, before a fire if possible, in case it be winter-time; and you may —such is my experience, and without this precaution I am a martyr to fleas—defy either flea, bug, or mosquito. It is quite a mistake to suppose that oiling one's self with sweet oil is a nasty, dirty operation. The oil sinks into the skin at once, and does not stain either cotton or linen."

He claims the same will render one generally insect-proof, and it might prove a protection against the black flies, midges, and other pests that mar the pleasure of touring in the Adirondacks, White Mountains,

Maine woods, etc., in the summer months. Some
hunting friends of mine who frequent those parts tell
me that they bathe all the exposed parts of the person
with *kerosene oil* three or four times a day, and find it
a complete safeguard. But the odor of this is offens-
ive to many.

Travelers have proverbially strange bed-fellows, and
few have knocked about the world for years without having met the plague of *lice*. These disgusting
creatures are of several distinct varieties. In Naples
one can see the lazzaroni picking one variety from each
other's hair and killing them; while in India those who
perform that friendly act place the insect carefully on
the ground, and would consider it a sin to injure it.
Rubbing the head with *kerosene oil*, and afterwards
washing it well, is the simplest treatment for these.

Those which inhabit the clothing — the familiar
"grayback" of our civil war—have a great antipathy
to *musk*, and if this is worn on the person, there is
little risk of receiving any of their visits.

How to Escape Malaria.

The newspapers, and doctors too, have had of
late years a great deal to say about *malaria*. This
term is often used incorrectly. Properly speaking,
a *malarial* disease means one which is charac-
terized by temporary suspensions, and then recur-
rences at regular intervals. Ague, or chills and fever,
remittent fever—that which in the South they call

"river fever," or "country fever"—are all malarial diseases. They prevail very extensively in this country
in the late summer and autumn, and every traveler
should be on his guard against them. If he is careful,
he can almost certainly escape them.

First, he must *live temperately.* There is a foolish
notion prevalent that whisky and tobacco will counter-
act malaria. Listen to what Dr. Martin says about
this, who is one of the standard English writers on the
hygiene of the tropics: "We hear much among certain classes of the supposed preventive influence of
spirits and cigars against night exposure, malaria and
contagion; but no medical observer, in any of our
numerous colonies, has ever seen reason to believe in
any such delusive doctrine, nor is there in reality the
slightest foundation for it."

Next, the clothing must not be *too light.* Avoid
linen, no matter how hot the weather. In India, a
long experience has proved the superiority of cotton
clothing in preventing the sudden chilling of the surface of the body by drafts and changing temperature.
Light silk or merino underwear is still better. During
some Indian expeditions, the surgeons noted the number of men who wore flannel next the skin and who did
not. The latter had invariably the highest sick and
death rates. Sailors learn this by experience. They
wear heavy flannel shirts even in tropical ports. A
large, loose outer garment is also exceedingly protective. The Spaniard wears his long cloak in winter to

keep himself warm; in summer, to keep himself cool.
If nothing more, at least adopt the oriental "khum-
merbund," which is imitated in India by Europeans in
the form of a silken, flannel or cotton waistband worn
next the skin.

A further warning is to *keep dry*. It is a false notion
that dampness is injurious only when it is cold. An
eminent physician, Dr. John Ordronaux, observes that
the further south we go the more protection do we
need against moisture, whether as dew, rain, or wet
feet.

The *night air* must be shunned. Physicians have
found that the malarial poison is most active for about
two hours after sunset and two hours before sunrise.
Not only is it more prudent to remain housed during
these hours, but the windows and doors should be
closed. In India the natives wrap their heads in their
clothes when sleeping in the night air. An open fire
is desirable, even when its warmth is not needed. The
sleeping quarters should be selected on as high ground
as possible, and on an upper story, as the malarial
poison is most intense in the lower strata of the air.

Great *fatigue* and anxiety lower the tone of the
system, and predispose to malaria. It is not always
possible for the traveler to escape them; but let him
remember their dangers.

Now I come to the real preventive of malarial fever.
It is *the daily use of quinine*, or some other preparation
of Peruvian bark. From three to five grains of qui-

nine taken every morning is almost a certain preventive, provided that reasonable prudence in other directions be observed. Pills containing this amount can be had of any manufacturing druggist, and should form part of the traveler's outfit.

To Avoid Taking Contagious Diseases.

Every one who journeys much will find himself occasionally exposed to infectious and contagious diseases. By some simple precautions, he can generally escape the influence of their poison. It is well known that many of them chiefly attack persons whose vital powers are already below par, through fatigue, exhaustion, or intemperance. These he should guard against. Cleanliness is a strong defence. Frequent bathing and changing of clothing should be observed. Avoid kissing, eating or drinking with a sick person. Do not enter the room on an empty stomach, if possible. It is well ascertained that at such a time persons are most apt to absorb infection. If necessarily exposed to a contagious disease for some time, take a brisk walk or ride in the open air, change your clothes and bathe on returning home. Sir Henry Holland, M. D., himself a remarkable traveler, relates that once, on the Black Sea, circumstances forced him to visit some peasants dying in their foul homes of the terrible pestilential plague fever of that locality. Immediately on leaving them he mounted his horse and galloped briskly for an hour in the pure air, and to this he attributed his escape from the infection. A dose of quinine (five or six grains) is also a useful safeguard after these exposures.

When, as in camp or at stations, one is obliged to live in an infectious atmosphere, the free use of *disinfectants* becomes imperative.

THE BEST DISINFECTANTS.

Sunlight, fresh air, soap and water, thorough cleanliness—for general use.

For special purposes the following are the most efficient, the simplest, and the cheapest.

1. *Copperas Disinfectant.*—Sulphate of iron (copperas), one and one-half pounds; water, one gallon.

A convenient way to prepare this is to suspend a basket containing about sixty pounds of copperas in a barrel of water. The solution should be frequently and liberally used in cellars, privies, water-closets, gutters, sewers, cess-pools, yards, stables, etc.

2. *Sulphur Disinfectant.*—Roll sulphur (brimstone), two pounds.

To a room ten feet square, and in the same proportion for larger rooms. Burn on an open vessel and shut up the room for twenty-four hours.

3. *Zinc Disinfectant.*—Sulphate of zinc (white vitriol), one and one-half pounds; common salt, three-quarters of a pound; water, six gallons.

For disinfecting discharges, cess-pools, etc.

4. *Thymol Water.*—Made by adding one tablespoonful *Spirits of Thymol* to half a gallon of water. Spirits

of thymol is composed of thymol, one ounce; alcohol, 85 per cent., three ounces.

May be used for all the disinfectant purposes of carbolic acid; it is quite as efficient in this strength, and has an agreeable odor. Where thymol is not available, chloride of zinc may be used—half an ounce of chloride of zinc to one gallon of water.

Sleeplessness.

A wise medical writer has said: "Whatever we detract from the requisite periods of our natural sleep, will surely be deducted in the end from the natural range of our existence."

Unfortunately, with many it is not a matter of choice. *Insomnia* is a horrid fiend which pursues them. I have very little faith in the various mental anodynes—repeating the alphabet, listening to reading, counting backwards, counting your breathing, etc. They may answer in light cases, but are worthless in real insomnia. Dr. Benjamin Franklin's resource was to arise, shake up his bed, walk around the room, and go to bed again. Dr. Duckworth recommends that before lying down one should use the flesh-brush freely, and bathe the face with cold water; and repeat this if wakefulness comes on during the night.

I cannot approve of opium, morphia, chloral, or spirits, for the purpose of inducing sleep in simple insomnia. They are apt to induce conditions which in the end are more distressing than the sleeplessness.

But I do not see any reasonable objection to the moderate use of *bromide of potassium.* There is no danger of forming the habit of taking it, it leaves no permanent effects, and it is not dangerously poisonous even in large quantities. In this opinion I am supported by the words of an eminent London physician in the *British Medical Journal,* who says:

"In summer, on the Continent, night-trains are the quickest and the coolest; and I have often enabled very weak and nervous women to travel all night without damage to health, by giving them 25 or 30 grains of bromide on starting, and the same dose on going to bed the following day, as soon after reaching their destination as possible. The first dose generally brings on the usual bromide sleep; or, at all events, it calms the system, and abates the irksome weariness of body and soul that follows long traveling in a cramped position. I have permitted patients to take the bromide in this way for two or three successive days, at a week's interval, during a two months' tour, warning them against taking large doses, and against taking the drug day after day during the whole course of traveling without further medical advice. This use of bromides I commend to the attention of the country practitioners who send us patients. If they come to us fatigued by a long journey, exhausted by a bad night, and by not having been able to breakfast, there is an aggravation of some of the symptoms of the case, which may mar the accuracy of our prognosis. If the complaint be slight, and the journey of moderate length, from 25 to 30 grains of bromide, taken on going to bed, will probably give sleep, and insure a quiet state of the system on the following morning. Should the case be serious, and the journey long, the same dose should be given at starting, and also on arriving. No doubt the journey to town will sometimes seriously aggravate the state of those who come up for advice; and I know nothing better calculated to prevent this than giving the bromide in the way I have described. Liquid medicines are objectionable in carpet-bags; but it is easy to have the roughly powdered bromide made up into powders of 20 or 30 grains each, one of which can be taken in half a glass of water."

Other soothing remedies, of value and practically harmless, are *Hoffman's anodyne* and the *elixir of valerianate of ammonia.* Either can be obtained at any well-stocked drug store, with directions.

Travelers are more liable to sleeplessness in some countries than in others. Thus I read the following in an article by Dr. David Young, an English practitioner at Florence.

" There is one circumstance which frequently causes anxiety to newcomers in Italy—*the want of sleep.* Almost every one goes through some experience of this kind, and invariably a brief sojourn sees this sleeplessness disappear. No drugs need as a rule be resorted to, and the traveler, if he is sensible and takes matters patiently, will not only find that his sleep re-

3

turns, but that he can do with very much less sleep
than in England, and that after what he would call a
sleepless night, he rises more refreshed than he used to
do at home after a longer and profounder sleep. This
is an important matter, and ignorance on the point
has more than once caused needless alarm to travelers."

Another plague of some persons is *nightmare*, which
especially afflicts them in traveling on account of
changing beds and surroundings. Those who visit
the tropics are also peculiarly liable to it. Generally
speaking, it is connected with some digestive disturbance. The most efficacious remedy is to take one
scruple (20 grains) of *bicarbonate of soda* in some pep-
permint water, on going to bed.

Sunstroke and Heatstroke.

During the summer that I passed in Calcutta, I
often saw the temperature at 105° in the shade, and
sunstroke was fearfully destructive of the foreign popu-
lation. Much of this fatality was owing to the careless
habits and self-indulgence of the sufferers. Thus I
noticed the ship captains who drank spirits freely died
in far greater proportion than the common sailors who
were restricted in this indulgence.

Special hats, made of pith about an inch thick, and
set off from the head on reed rests, so as to allow a
free circulation of air over the skull, are much used
in India, and are valuable protectors. In Australia,

where the temperature at Christmas is frequently over 110°, a light muslin turban is twisted into a rope, and rolled around the hat. A bunch of fresh green leaves in the crown of the hat is a popular and sensible device in our hot American summers. Dr. Wood says that the free use of cool water as a beverage in summer is to be recommended as a preventive of sunstroke, as it keeps up the action of the skin by promoting perspiration.

When a person exposed to intense heat begins to feel giddy and slightly sick, with perhaps a headache, or feeling of pressure on the brain, he is in danger, and should at once seek the shade, open his clothing to the air, and bathe his head and neck assiduously in cold or ice water. It is unwise to take spirits, but some cold tea or coffee, drawn strong, will be very grateful.

Should the case have gone further, and should he have dropped insensible, then the directions are to loosen his clothing, place him with head and shoulders a little raised, and give him a cold douche, and plenty of it, by pouring jug after jug of water from the height of three or four feet on the top of his head and down his spine; or better, apply an ice-bag, if you can get it, to the head. Sponge also his hands, feet and chest with cold water. Keep him in a darkened room, and where, if possible, there is a nice draft, and let him be *perfectly quiet* and undisturbed. If he seems likely to sink altogether, put a blister or a mustard poultice

on the nape of the neck, and administer strong beef-
tea, or strong brandy and water, slowly, by an enema.

In St. Louis, they have had good success in using
warm water instead of cold, a hot mustard bath bring-
ing about reaction they claim more satisfactorily than
the cold.

In India many surgeons have adopted the plan of
injecting quinine under the skin, which they report
has succeeded better than any other treatment.

Poisonous Bites and Stings.

Spirits of ammonia (spirits of hartshorn) is the standard application for the stings of bees, wasps, hornets,
etc.   It should be diluted with twice its bulk of water
and applied to the part.   When it is not at hand, as it
rarely is, some *bicarbonate of soda* may be rubbed up
with water and laid on the part; or it may be washed
with a strong solution of it.   This is also a first-rate
application in *burns*, scalds, and in poisoning by *poison
ivy*, or *poison oak*.

Simpler remedies are to rub the bitten spot with a
raw onion, or the end of a cigar, or plug well-chewed;
or to place upon it a poultice of wet clay.

If the bite is that of a venomous serpent, suck the
wound immediately, tie a string tightly around the
limb between the wound and the body, and bathe the
injured spot with water containing as much spirits of
ammonia as the patient can bear

Diarrhœa and Constipation.

The change of food and water is very apt to dis-turb the action of the bowels in traveling, producing either constipation or diarrhœa. Especially is the latter apt to occur in hot weather.

It is well not to medicate much for it. Dr. Francis Galton, who is good authority, recommends that nothing be taken but broth or rice. Others find the " dry diet," that is, eating but little solid food and en-tirely abstaining from liquids, to produce rapid relief. When such simple measures do not answer, a dose of castor oil will frequently remove irritating substances and be better than beginning with astringents.

Of medicines, the common *paregoric elixir*, a tea-spoonful two or three times a day, or the *chalk mix-ture* of the pharmacists, are valuable preparations. A very excellent combination is the following:

```
Diluted sulphuric acid . . . . . . . . . . . . 15 drops.
Laudanum. . . . . . . . . . . . . . . . . . . 10   "
Essence of ginger . . . . . . . . . . . . . . 20   "
Cinnamon or peppermint water . . . . . . . . 1 ounce.
```

To be taken at one dose and repeated every two or three hours till relief is obtained.

The *constipation* from which many suffer in traveling can most generally be relieved by diet. Oat meal, corn grits, cracked wheat, figs, dates, fresh ripe fruit, and the like, will usually enable one to dispense with medicines. A tumbler of water before breakfast is of use.

If these measures are inadequate, some of the laxative mineral waters now so readily attainable may be employed, as the Friedrichshall, Saratoga, Geyser or Congress, Hunyadi, etc.

Of drugs, the least objectionable are castor oil and rhubarb, as these do not leave a habit of constipation after them. One to three grains of rhubarb may be taken after each meal, or once daily, as required.

Catching Cold.

The remedy for a *commencing cold*, which long experience has proved to be worth all others, is a full dose of *opium* in some form, either 30 or 40 drops of laudanum (or, what is better, McMunn's elixir), or $\frac{1}{8}$ or $\frac{1}{4}$ grain of morphia, or one or two grains of pure gum opium, just as is convenient. It must be taken early in the disease, and no particular care about diet or housing one's self need be observed. Repeat if required.

Some persons, however, cannot bear opium in any form. It makes them dreadfully sick. For these I have used and recommend 20 or 30 drops of the muriated tincture of iron taken in plenty of water; or a teaspoonful of the ammoniated tincture of guaiacum; or 20 or 30 drops of tincture of belladonna. Any of these will promptly break up a commencing cold in most cases.

If the cold has had several days' start, and has passed into a bronchitis, " settled on the chest," as people say, then the above measures are of no use, and might, indeed, be injurious. For such a condition, especially when there is some feverishness, a feeling of soreness and tightness across the breast, and a dry irritating cough, go to bed in a warmed room, and take the following powder after you are in bed:

Dover's powder . . . . 10 grains,
Quinine . . . . 5 grains.
For one dose.

This, especially if accompanied by a glass of *hot* lemonade, will produce free perspiration.

There are any number of cough mixtures. I have found the following as useful as any. Take

Syrup of ipecac,
Syrup of squills,
Paregoric elixir, equal parts.
Dose. A teaspoonful three to six times a day as needed.

A light mustard plaster on the chest is often efficient in removing soreness, and hastening recovery.

Sore Throat.

This very common complaint in our climate is often aggravated by exposure in traveling. The popular remedy is *chlorate of potash*. This is obtainable in the form of "compressed pellets" at most drug stores, and a box of them should form part of the voyager's baggage. They are often sufficient, and are certainly most handy to use.

But where there is decided inflammation of the

throat, with swelling of the tonsils, and pain in swallowing, I advise prompt recourse to what I consider the true specific remedy in this disease, and that is *guaiacum.* The ammoniated tincture is the most convenient form and I use in preference the following gargle. Take

Ammoniated tincture of guaiacum . . . . ½ ounce,
Liquor of potassa . . . . 1 drachm,
Cinnamon water . . . . 4 ounces.
For a gargle. Use about two teaspoonfuls at a time, every hour or two.

I have rarely failed to cure an inflammatory sore throat with this, inside of twenty-four hours.

Persons much subject to sore throat should bathe the throat outside with cold water every morning, and gargle with a tumbler of cold water containing a teaspoonful of tincture of myrrh.

Toothache.

If the traveler prepares himself for his journey as I have suggested at the opening of this book, he will not be likely to be afflicted with toothache. But as he will meet others who are not so wise, he may recommend them to begin with a dose of salts, aperient mineral water, or other laxative medicine; as soon as this operates, in all probability the pain will be gone for a week or two. Meanwhile, apply a small mustard poultice outside, just over the place where the pain is most violent, and rub the gum and the tooth

with chloroform and laudanum mixed. If the tooth
be a hollow one and very painful, then put in the
cavity a little cotton-wool dipped in chloroform and
laudanum. It will ease the dreadful pain. A little
bit of cotton dipped in a solution of shellac, or of gum
mastic and spirits of wine, makes a good temporary
filling for very bad teeth. Creasote is the safest domestic remedy to employ, if the pain be very bad; it
is used by putting a little bit of cotton-wool dipped in
it into the hollow of the tooth. Do not try to put it
in for yourself, or you will scarify your tongue and
gums.

Mr. Turner, an English writer, says in a recent
book: "The following remedy for toothache was
given me by a dentist of very great reputation: 'First
wash the mouth well with warm water; then use the
following tincture: Tannin, ten grains; gum mastic,
one-half drachm; ten drops of carbolic acid; dissolve
in half an ounce of sulphuric ether.' Paint the de-
cayed hollow of the aching tooth over with this, twice,
or even thrice, using a camel's-hair brush. I have
never found it to fail; and I have used it myself
some hundreds of times, both at sea and on shore.
The remedy will last good a month or more. Then
apply it again if the pain returns: it does not hurt the
other teeth. Take care and keep the tincture in a vial
with a glass stopper—not a cork, as the gum mastic
makes the cork stick fast in the neck of the vial, and
break."

3*

Hiccough.

This is to some people a distressing annoyance, and appears sometimes to be produced by the jolting motion of the cars. With some it may be checked by pressing the point of the finger firmly on the center of the upper lip. But the most reliable remedy is *pounded ice* or *ice cream.* Few hiccoughs from any cause will resist a plate of the latter agreeable compound.

Earache.

For simple cases, the result of exposure to cold, a hot mush poultice will usually relieve the pain. The domestic remedy of a roast onion, wrapped in flannel, and applied to the ear as hot as it can be borne, is even better. The habit of stuffing the ears with cotton is a bad one, and should be avoided. (See also p. 61.)

Nose Bleed.

This unpleasant accident often occurs to children on journeys. Ice to the back of the neck, and stretching the hands and arms in a straight line above the body will generally check it. Snuffing up tannic acid is also efficacious, and when persons are subject to such attacks it is well to have this drug along.

Vertigo or Dizziness.

Many persons are constitutionally subject to this on ascending a height or on looking downward. To a traveler it is an exceedingly inconvenient weakness, and those who are liable to it should not attempt to make important mountain climbs, or to expose themselves to crossing narrow bridges, etc. There is no certain prevention of it. Some have succeeded in overcoming the tendency by accustoming themselves first to moderate heights, and then to greater ones. The affection is purely mental. If the mind can be steadily occupied with other thoughts, and the gaze directed upwards or horizontally, the dizziness will not appear.

This variety of vertigo is by no means the same as that from which many are habitual sufferers. This latter is generally of dyspepsia, and is often brought on by the use of tobacco or coffee to excess. By reducing or omitting the use of them, it will frequently disappear.

Suggestions about Medicines.

A traveler does not want to carry a trunk-full of drugs; but there are a few which it is very wise for him to have with him for immediate use, and when remote from drug stores. Their choice depends a good deal on where he is going and the nature of his business. Leaving these special considerations to him, I would name the following as of service on all journeys of length :

Bromide of potash. This has been already mentioned (page 48). As I have said, it is most conveniently carried in powders of thirty grains each. One

two or three of these may be taken at intervals. It
soothes the system, relieves nervous headache, lessens
the irritability of the stomach, overcomes sleeplessness,
and has no permanent bad effects.

Opium or morphia. These extremely valuable preparations have some serious objections. The habit of
taking opium, either in the form of laudanum or morphia, or of smoking the gum, Chinese fashion, is a
most deplorable one. But as a medicinal agent, opium
occupies the first rank. Taken early, it checks the
ill-effects of exposure to cold, relieves pain, induces
sleep, and soothes nervous irritability. The average
dose of gum opium for an adult (children do not bear
it well), is one grain ; this equals a quarter of a grain
of morphia, or twenty drops of laudanum. One must
remember, in using it, that it is a poison, and that repeating such doses may be dangerous.

Paregoric, a popular and excellent remedy for loose-
ness of the bowels, contains one grain of opium to the
ounce, combined with useful stomachics.

Mustard is the most convenient and effective coun-
ter-irritant. The mustard paper or prepared mustard
plasters to be found in any first-class drug store are
cleanly, and occupy little room, while they are an excellent remedy for pains and aches.

Quinine is indispensable to the traveler in malarious
regions; as a preventive of malaria I have already
spoken of three or five grains once a day ; but if a chill
has been experienced, that much should be taken three

or four times a day.   Pills can be bought, containing three grains each, which are handy to carry.

Chloroform is especially useful for the immediate relief of pain.   A few drops of it on a handkerchief, and occasionally inhaled, will often relieve a headache and dispel the nausea of sea-sickness or the motion of a car.   The following mixture is most excellent for *earache*:

Chloroform . . . . 1 drachm,
Olive oil . . . . 1 ounce.
Mix and shake well together.   Then pour 20 or 30 drops into the ear, and close it up with a piece of raw cotton.

Extract of beef, now to be had of excellent quality, put up in tins, is well worth having with one when invalids are in the party.   A gill, nicely warmed, will act as a delightful stimulant, and in fatiguing journeys, or when meals are not to be had regularly, it is an excellent substitute for substantial food.

These are the medicinal preparations which the traveler will find most useful, and he will generally meet with some emergency in which one or other of them will be welcome.